Table of Contents

ISBN 9780578523064

All Scripture references are from the King James
Version of the Bible

Rear Cover Photograph by John DiRoma

Acknowledgements

Well, I did it. I wrote a book. At first, I suppose my intentions were simply therapeutic. My own deep personal convictions needed an outlet. But as I shared my thoughts with friends and family, I found encouragement to make it into a book.

Gordon G. Goertz, Jr., one of my friends of longest tenure, (I would say one of my *oldest friends*, but, well, you know), you were the first to read my manuscript. I appreciate your candid critique of the writing. But what I appreciate most is you telling me that the content would be encouraging to pastors. You gave me the confidence to go ahead with the project.

To Charles (Chuck) Leiss (the unofficial president of my fan club), my sincere thanks. You let me know that readers would be able to sense the spirit in which the book was written. I'm grateful for the sessions of "lunch therapy" where I was able to vent my feelings. I know you were not aware at the time, but you were helping me think through much of what is written in this book. Thank you for your friendship.

To Joanne Mazzotta, my friend from Reservoir Avenue, thank you. It is amazing how God orchestrates His divine plan. Never would I have dreamed that a neighbor from the old block would one day be so enheartening to me. As a published author, you were the first person from whom I sought advice. You were incredibly helpful and encouraging from the very beginning. Thank you for helping me to realize that I really could be an author.

To Deanna Joy, my little girl, my beautiful little baby (you will always be my little girl), thank you. You believed in me when others didn't think I was serious. I know you always have my six. I'm glad I have someone like you in my corner.

I am grateful to everyone who prays for me that I might continue to be faithful in the ministry of the Gospel of Jesus Christ.

Preface

For several years there have been many thoughts kicking around in my head and heart. I finally decided to sit down and commit them to paper. I've always thought that it was presumptuous on my part to write a book. I mean, unless someone has walked on the moon, won multiple Super Bowls, or something similarly incredible, who really cares what they have to say? But the more I thought about it, the more I believed that perhaps the Lord has given me this desire for a reason. I know I am not the only pastor who feels the way I feel about the subject. Maybe, just maybe some other pastor of a small church will read this and be encouraged. If that should happen, I praise God for the opportunity to have been of help.

Some may say, "You're only saying these things because you pastor a small church. You would be speaking differently if your church was larger." And they would be right. I would be. But I don't pastor a large church, and I don't believe I ever will. Please understand that I do not intend to criticize large churches or their pastors. I do not mean to suggest that if a church is large, they must be doing something wrong. I have attended several large churches, even mega-churches over the years where the Spirit of God was moving greatly. My intention rather is to consider the goal with which we approach our ministry calling. Not all churches are going to be mega-churches. I do not believe God intends them all to be.

The fact is most Evangelical churches in the US are considered small churches. I am not a statistics guy. What I mean is that I don't live by statistics. But in the research that I have done I have discovered that as a pastor of a small church, I am in the majority. According to many recent surveys, the size of the average Protestant church in America is less than one hundred adults. Only 2% of American Christian churches have over 1000 adults attending.

There is a lot of reliance on statistics in the Church Growth Movement. When I was in secular management, statistics were important to me. I realize there is a place for demographics, surveys, and crunching of numbers in the corporate world and marketing. I would also agree that they may have a place somewhere in church leadership discussions. But, as I said, I'm not governed by statistics.

I am not saying that studying statistics is

unspiritual. But when it comes to the ministry of God's Bride, the Church, our reliance must be on the leading of the Holy Spirit, and not on statistical analysis. I care little about the superficial. All that really matters is what God has to say.

This is written for the pastor of the small church who has decided to not give up no matter how difficult it may be. For the pastor who has determined to not compromise, who will not rely on the arm of the flesh. It is written, hopefully, to be an encouragement to the faithful who have become or are becoming discouraged.

Pastors of small churches are not considered successful in the modern church world. We are rarely invited to speak at conventions. Seldom are we asked what we might be doing in ministry. Perhaps the occasional breakout session at the annual men's or women's conference, but probably not the keynote speaker. If our churches aren't growing, no one wants to hear what we have to say.

Some of the most devoted and committed men and women I know are pastors of small churches. Every day they faithfully pray and prepare the Word for their congregations. In my view, they are the real heroes.

I know the small church pastor is often looked upon like *The Little Engine That Could*. You know, "Come on, you could do it." The fact is, no, we can't do it. We were never intended to do it. God could if He chooses to. But that is entirely up to Him. In light of the fact that the greater majority of churches in America are considered small churches, it would appear that God might view things differently

I pray this book is an encouragement. That is all it is intended to be.

Today's Expectations

Something has happened to the church world in the last twenty years or so. It is what has come to be known as the "Church Growth Movement." Perhaps this philosophy was there right along, but I was not aware of it. I came to the saving knowledge of Jesus Christ in 1981 at the age of twenty-one. I was brought to Christ by a couple of friends who were sincerely concerned for my eternal soul. They weren't trying to bring me to church necessarily. They were trying to bring me to Christ. In listening to them talk and by watching their lives, I came to the realization that I was missing something very important in my life. I didn't have the peace they had, or the joy. I didn't have the assurance of my sins being forgiven. When I was confronted with the gospel, I knew what was missing. When I was made aware of the holy standard of God's Righteousness and compared it to my sinful lifestyle, I came up way short. I confessed my sin to God and received His forgiveness through His Son, Jesus Christ.

I was not a number to be added to their church

roster. I was a soul they felt they needed to rescue. And I was rescued.

The Lord led me to a wonderful church. They were meeting in a public-school auditorium while a new church building was going up. The church was growing. There was great excitement about being part of that fellowship. I often say that I was afraid to miss a service because I didn't want to miss what God was doing. If I had to work and couldn't be in church for a service, I would call my friends after work to find out how church went. It never failed, someone got saved, someone received healing, there was prayer time at the altar and folks got delivered from burdens they had been carrying, etc. I don't know what your church background is, or what your church experiences have been, but the church I went to was exciting! There was no special lighting, no smoke machines, no professional musical performances, just people who loved God, a pastor who preached the Word of God without compromise, the whole counsel of God, and the anointing of the Holy Spirit. And the church was growing, in a school auditorium.

When I say church was exciting, I don't just mean for me. I was a single young man in my early twenties. I was surrounded by my peers who were just as excited about God as I was. We were in church Sunday morning, Sunday evening, Tuesday night for the church prayer meeting, Thursday night for Bible Study, and we hung out together on Friday and Saturday nights. We would go out for lunch or dinner together after or between services.

There were times when an evening service would go late into the night. No one wanted to leave. Even after the lights went out, and the doors were closed, people would gather in the church parking lot, just talking about what God was doing in their lives.

Young families would bring their children dressed in their pajamas. The children would fall asleep while the service went on, and they would be carried out of church, to home, and right into bed. Parents didn't use their young children as an excuse to stay home from church. Kids literally grew up in church. A large number of those children that I watched grow up in church are now involved in some ministry or service to the Lord.

This wasn't just happening in the church I attended. There was a hunger in the hearts of people for God. Many churches that I was familiar with were experiencing the same thing. Young people, old people, and everyone in between. Not once did I hear of a church growth seminar.

When I went to Bible college, I found a similar environment. God was moving amongst His church. Each class would begin with a student-led devotion with each student having their turn bringing the devotion. I remember several times when our classroom became church. For example, in a basic College Math class, one of my fellow students opened the class with a devotion. I don't recall the message, but what I do remember clearly is that the Holy Spirit's presence was overwhelming. Everyone in the classroom was moved by God's presence. There were students kneeling at their school desks, weeping before God, surrendering their lives to Him in repentance and worship. The bell rang, and the class was over. We made our way to the daily chapel service where the service opened with worship, and the Sanctuary was filled with the presence of the Lord. Again, I do not recall who the preacher was, or what they had to say, but when the altar call was given, nearly the entire student body, and most of the college professors made their way to the altar, or as near to the altar as the crowd would allow. God was moving in the lives of His people, and we were rejoicing in His presence. The president of the college came to the platform to announce that classes would be cancelled for the remainder of the day to give us the freedom to stay before the Lord in prayer. This happened quite often in my time at Bible College.

I often look back to those days with longing. Never did it cross my mind that this which we were experiencing might only be for a season. Perhaps I took for granted that this was what Christianity was, and would always be. It was this way when I first came to Christ. It was this way in the church I attended. It was this way in the churches around me. It was this way in Bible College. This is what it was to be a Christian. It could only get better.

I don't know what the factors were. Was it just that God was blessing the faithfulness of those men and women of God who pastored, and taught, and evangelized? Did they find favor with God? Was God blessing the spiritual hunger within my peers and me? Was it simply a matter of the sovereignty of God moving in His perfect timing? Was it all the above? What was it that made our spiritual lives so fulfilling, and our church experience so rewarding? What were we doing or not doing that God was blessing? I still don't have the answer. All I know is that something changed. Gradually, and almost undetected, there was a change. Something was missing. There wasn't the same excitement of being in church. People got busy with their lives. Families became absorbed with Little League, soccer games, dance recitals, and just about any kind of preoccupation. Church attendance began to dwindle. So, what do we do? Something. Anything. Enter the evolution of the Church Growth Movement.

The church got desperate. As they say, "Desperate

times call for desperate measures." I have read of the desperation in the hearts of men and women of God in times past. When there was a deep longing for the holy presence of God many books were written. For instance, the writings of A.W. Tozer such as *The Knowledge of the Holy, The Pursuit of God*, and *The Fellowship of the Burning Heart*. Or those written by Watchman Nee like *A Living Sacrifice*. Or E.M. Bounds' *Power Through Prayer*. Or Andrew Murray's *Waiting on God*; Hanna Whitall Smith's *The God of All Comfort*; Smith Wigglesworth's *Faith That Prevails*; Jonathan Edwards' *A Call to United Extraordinary Prayer*. Compare this list to the list of the top ten church growth books. "How to...," "Five Practices of...," "Six steps to…" It puzzles me why when there are so many books written by men and women who saw great moves of God in years past, the church would spend time looking for something new. It reminds me of the philosophers Paul debated on Mars Hill in Athens, Greece. They "spent their time in nothing else, but either to tell, or to hear some new thing." (Acts 17:21b).

In I Kings chapter 12 we read the story of Rehoboam, King of Israel. He was the son of Solomon and reigned after Solomon died. He consulted with the elders of Israel who counseled him in the best ways to gain the respect and service of the people. But

Rehoboam rejected the counsel of the elders and listened to the counsel of his peers. This ultimately led to the division of the Northern and Southern kingdoms. The counsel of the elders would have conceivably led to the unity of God's people rather than division. But Rehoboam chose the modern ways over the ways of wisdom, and he did so with tragic results.

And in all this new counsel being developed by the Church Growth Movement, the church in America continues to be in decline. It is true that there are churches that are growing. Some are growing as they adhere to the Great Commission, and souls are being added to the church as they are translated from darkness to light. Jesus said the gates of hell would not prevail against His church (Matthew 16:18). But I see another trend, as well. What I refer to as the *big box churches*.

In the New England town where I was born there was a hardware store in the town center. It opened in 1783 just after the American Revolution. It closed in 1999 after 216 years of service to the community. You could always find what you needed at the local hardware store. The staff was always ready and willing to help with just about any project one might have, offering their years of accumulated knowledge and experience. Then a big box home improvement store moved into town. It wasn't long before our local hardware store was forced to close. They could not compete with the marketing strategies of the big box store.

I have seen this same trend in the church world, not only as it effects the congregation I presently pastor, but the congregations of many of my peers. I hope I do not come across as bitter, because I certainly am not. But I do wish to point out a truth which is perhaps being overlooked. There are churches boasting in their church growth, but at the expense of the loss to others. Unless church growth comes by way of conversions, it isn't growth at all. It is merely migration.

Before coming to the church I now pastor, I was asked by two other churches to consider being their pastor. I live in New England which is notorious for having smaller churches. The first church was down to fifteen adults in their Sunday morning worship service. I asked the representative from their Church Board about their history. "Was there a time when your attendance was greater than it is now?" He informed me that their attendance had been averaging seventy-five adults on a Sunday morning. Some changes had taken place, and sixty people had left. As I spoke with the Board Member from the second church, I was informed that they were proudly a "growing church," and they had recently doubled in size. Their current attendance was approximately 120 people. I realized by looking at a map that they were within driving distance of one another. Do the math. Sixty people leaving one church to attend another church is not church growth.

What exactly *is* church growth?

A neighboring pastor once asked me if I had a Sunday evening service, and what the attendance might be. He told me there were people in his church that wanted to go deeper in the things of God, but he didn't have anything like that for them. He said that he "Aimed for the middle" because that is what most people want. His concern was growing his church.

When this attitude exists, the results are often large churches made up of church members who have no moral moorings. It is clear in the modern media. Recently there have been some high visibility Christians who were given platforms on national TV. When asked about issues that are clearly unbiblical, these people folded like lawn chairs. It appears they were more concerned with being politically correct than biblically correct. The modern church culture is mass-producing Christians who have little to no biblical knowledge.

The middle. Jesus rebuked the church in Laodicea for being lukewarm (Revelation 3:16). He said He would rather them be either hot or cold. It is often taught that Jesus was saying regarding being cold that if they were not going to be *on fire* for God, He would rather they be cold rather than to be indifferent. That makes no sense at all. In what sense would the Lord want anyone to be cold in relation to the things of God? He was referring to the motivation of the people of the Laodicean church. The church was being weakened by the culture around them. The city felt they were self-sufficient and needed nothing. Laodicea was boasting in their production of soft, black wool, healing eye salve, and their banking institutions. Laodicea had a serious water problem. Unlike the water of Hierapolis and Colossae, Laodicea's mineral-laden, lukewarm water was sickening. Hierapolis, which is present day Pamukkale, Turkey was known for its hot mineral springs. People would travel for miles to bathe in its waters. The hot water and mineral content offered relief to various illnesses.

In contrast to the hot waters of Hierapolis are the cold springs of Colossae. The icy-cold water would flow down from the snow-covered peaks of Mount Cadmus offering the residents and travelers a refreshing source of water. The waters from Hierapolis and those from Colossae would meet at Laodicea. What Jesus was saying in His rebuke to the church there was that they had allowed the culture surrounding them to alter their reliance. Rather than looking to the Lord for their sufficiency they had come to rely upon their own resources. Instead of offering healing and comfort like the waters of Hierapolis, or providing refreshing like the waters of Colossae, their self-sufficient attitude was as distasteful as their water supply. They were lukewarm, therefore distasteful to the Lord. Not hot, not cold, but in the middle.

I have noticed recently several churches advertising themselves as "a church for people who don't like church." My friend, I love church! I've always loved church. I was saved in church. I met my wife in church. Most of my friends came from church. God called me to the ministry while in church. There is nothing at all wrong with church. I want our church to be a church for people who love church. God loves the church. We *are* the church.

Today's expectation is that all churches must be growing in size or they are dead or dying. That may be the case for some. But that most certainly is not the case across the board. When Jesus spoke to His disciples just prior to His Ascension, He gave them this assignment we know as the Great Commission. In Matthew's account of the gospel, Jesus said, "All power is given unto me in heaven and in earth. Go ye therefore, and teach all nations, baptizing them in the name of the Father, and of the Son, and of the Holy Ghost: Teaching them to observe all things whatsoever I have commanded you: and, lo, I am with you alway, even unto the end of the world. Amen." (Matthew 28:18b-20). In Mark's gospel account Jesus is recorded as saying, "… preach the gospel to every creature." (Mark 16:16). This commission is to be obeyed by all Jesus' followers of every generation. The mission? Preach the gospel to everyone and teach those who receive His word. He never assigned us the task of building His church. In fact, that work He reserves for Himself. Jesus said, "… and upon this rock *I will build My church*; and the gates of hell shall not prevail against it." (Matthew 16:18b).

Jesus said when the Holy Spirit came His disciples would be witnesses of Him starting where they were, and everywhere they went (Acts 1:8). On the Day of Pentecost, after the Holy Spirit had descended upon His disciples, they preached the gospel as commissioned. The results? *"And the Lord added to the church* daily such as should be saved." (Acts 2:47).

Being Filled with the Spirit

What was Jesus saying when He gave His disciples the Great Commission? When He said that all power was given to Him, He was referring to His victory over death and hell. He was referring to the glory that was His from eternity past, now restored after His resurrection. He was now authorizing them; empowering them to carry out the Father's will. "Go ye therefore..." I was taught to always ask what *therefore* is there for. "I have all authority, consequently you are to go and preach and to teach all people." (Matthew 28:18-20). He promised to be with them as they went.

Before they were to go, they were to wait. Jesus promised to send the necessary power. He never expected His disciples, then or now to attempt to respond to His call in their own abilities. It is impossible to do the supernatural by natural means. If we put together what Jesus said in Luke 24:47-50, Acts 1:8, and Matthew 28:18-20, we will better understand the Great Commission. "I have sent you under My authority. I will give you all the power necessary to accomplish the task I assigned you. I will be with you the entire time. You have no need to worry or fear."

Here is the problem. The modern church is looking for another way. E.M. Bounds said it best when he said, "The church is looking for better methods; God is looking for better men"[1]. I understand him to mean men and women of a greater commitment. The church is looking for a shortcut. It has become a lot more work than it has to be. Ministry was never supposed to be so difficult. Jesus said, "Take my yoke upon you, and learn of me; for I am meek and lowly in heart: and ye shall find rest unto your souls. For my yoke is easy, and my burden is light." (Matthew 11:29-30).

The Church Growth Movement is, in a large measure attempting to lean on the arm of the flesh. There is no shortage of new church programs or paradigms. No shortage of seminars or instructional videos. I have been to many seminars as have many of my friends. Pretty much every time we came back to our small churches excited about "plugging in" the newly learned techniques or strategies. Pretty much every time it didn't work.

Of course, we could learn from one another, and we should share ideas and tips we have learned along the way. We should be willing to try new things and take chances within reason. My point is that we may be setting ourselves up for failure. It worked over there. Why doesn't it work over here? I have come to understand that God wants us to rely completely and absolutely on Him.

The psalmist wrote in Psalm 127:1, "Except the Lord build the house they labour in vain that build it: except the Lord keep the city, the watchman waketh but in vain." All the effort in the world will not result in a growing church if the Lord is not growing that church. I believe this is one cause of great frustration among pastors. I know it was for me.

The apostle Paul writing to the Ephesian church said, "And be not drunk with wine, wherein is excess; but be filled with the Spirit." (Ephesians 5:18). One becomes drunk, intoxicated by excessive alcohol consumption. It is the repeated or continuous consumption of wine that Paul sites as the opposite of what they should do. When one is drunk with wine, they are said to be *under the influence* of alcohol. It is the repeated or continual drinking that causes intoxication. Paul used the present passive imperative when writing "be filled" with the Spirt. It would be more clearly translated "be being filled with the Spirit", or "But be constantly controlled by the Spirit." We are to be constantly being filled with the Holy Spirit so that we are under the influence of the Holy Spirit. We are to be filled to the point of overflowing. It is out of the overflow that we minister to others. If we are not spending the necessary time in the presence of the Lord to be filled until we overflow, then we are attempting to minister from our own vessels. This is where burnout comes from. We become frustrated and discouraged trying to minister out of our own reserves rather than out of the spiritual abundance. We must be being filled with the Spirit.

In the book of Zechariah chapter 4, we are encouraged to rely on the Spirit's power. Zerubbabel was king of Judah. He was attempting to rebuild the Temple of the Lord. Joshua was the High Priest assisting him, and Zechariah was God's prophet. Zechariah was receiving a vision from the Lord. In the context, Joshua, the High Priest who represents Israel before God is standing before God in filthy rags. The rags represent the condition of our fallen race before a holy God. As Isaiah said, "But we are all as an unclean thing, and all our righteousnesses are as filthy rags; and we all do fade as a leaf; and our iniquities, like the wind, have taken us away." (Isaiah 64:6). Satan is standing there to resist Joshua. Satan is always resisting the work of the Lord. "But we are not ignorant of his devices." (II Cor. 2:11). If we put on the whole armor of God, we will be able to stand against the wiles of the devil (Eph. 6:11).

The rags were removed, and he was given clean

garments. The Lord rebuked Satan and gave Joshua clean robes. This is what Christ has done for us. He delivered us from the power of darkness and placed us in the Kingdom of Christ (Colossians 1:13). He has clothed us in robes of Righteousness (Isa. 61:1).

The angel awakened Zechariah out of sleep. The church has fallen asleep. In many cases we are simply sleepwalking; eyes wide open but not seeing, not discerning. I have read about people walking in their sleep, driving their cars, even committing crimes. It is possible to function while completely unaware.

The purpose of the church in the world is to be a lamp that gives light (Matthew 5:14). Years ago, this was the spirit that moved the church. Not so much anymore. Today the focus has shifted to growth, often marketing the church to meet the temporal needs of the community. The clear instruction from Jesus is that we should seek His kingdom and His Righteousness first and foremost. Our temporal needs would then be met by Him (Matthew 6:33). Being a light supersedes all other needs. In many circles, the "stuff" has become the main purpose. You cannot deny the fact that the modern church is not the church we read about in Scripture.

The church needs to wake up. The angel asked, "What do you see?" Let me ask you, do you see what's going on in our day? We are losing moral ground, and

I fear we may not get it back. We could curse the darkness, or we could be the light.

"What do you see?" In the vision, there is a lampstand with seven lamps. There is a bowl for a reservoir feeding the lamps, and two olive trees supplying the bowl. The angel asks Zechariah, "Don't you understand what you see?" "And he said, 'No, my lord." This is the story of the church today. We still don't understand. We keep trying everything else.

Zerubbabel was discouraged in the building of the temple. God was telling him that it wasn't about human endeavor. By way of the vision, He was giving His assurance that the responsibility of the task was not on his shoulders alone.

Oil is often a symbol of the Holy Spirit in Scripture. The pair of olive trees supplying the reservoir feeding the lamps was God's assurance that He would supply all that was needed for the building of the Temple. "This is the word of the Lord unto Zerubbabel, saying, 'Not by might, nor by power, but by My Spirit saith the Lord of hosts." The angel went on to say that the hands of Zerubbabel had started the work, and it would be his hands that would finish the work. But it would not be done *because of* his hands. It would be accomplished because the Lord, by His Spirit would enable Zerubbabel to fulfill the task. He then said, "For who hath despised the day of *small things?"*

When Paul was with the church in Corinth, he did not rely upon his own abilities. He was highly educated having sat under the tutelage of Gamaliel, one of the greatest doctors of the Jewish law of Paul's day (Acts 5:34; 22:3). Writing to the Corinthian church regarding his time spent with them, Paul said, "And I, brethren, when I came to you, came not with excellency of speech or of wisdom, declaring unto you the testimony of God. For I determined not to know any thing among you, save Jesus Christ, and him crucified. And I was with you in weakness, and in fear, and in much trembling. And my speech and my preaching was not with enticing words of man's wisdom, but in demonstration of the Spirit and of power: That your faith should not stand in the wisdom of men, but in the power of God" (I Cor. 2:1-5).

Paul's reliance was not upon his oratory skills or his ability to debate the culture of his day. He wasn't concerned with being *relevant.* His message was redemption through Christ. His reliance was upon the Spirit's power being demonstrated through his preaching. No one would be able to say that Paul built the church in Corinth.

This doesn't mean that we are not to do our best to learn new things and apply wisdom and knowledge. We could always do more to better ourselves and our ministry efforts. Confucius said, "The expectations of life depend upon diligence; the mechanic that would perfect his work must first sharpen his tools." So, sharpen your tools. But remember that we are His tools. Perhaps He is using our struggles to sharpen us.

Being A Shepherd

I sat on a hillside in the Black Forest in Germany one afternoon in the 1980s. I was living in a Bible School in Erzhausen while studying in a language school in Darmstadt. I would head south on weekends. Germany is absolutely beautiful, especially the Black Forest region. I would often just take in the beauty of the countryside.

There aren't any sheep in the town where I grew up. At least, none I am aware of. But there on the hillside in Germany, there were sheep. Lots of them. The odd thing is that they each had a number printed in their fleece. I was told that there was a large industrial sheep farm up the road from where I was sitting. The sheepherders were actually employees of the farm and used the numbers to keep track of the sheep that were assigned to them. They would literally count sheep. I watched as the herders would move the sheep where they wanted them to go. Most of the time they were behind them yelling to drive the sheep ahead. Being a city boy, I didn't think much of it. That is until I met a gentleman who owned a small flock of sheep. He lived in a little village in the same area. What struck me most was that he wasn't behind his sheep yelling to drive them anywhere. He was in front of them, and they were following him. In fact, they wanted to go everywhere he went. When he went inside his home, he had to shut the gate behind him to keep them from following him inside. They were *his* sheep, and he was their shepherd. There was no need to number them in order to keep track of them. He knew each one, and each one knew him.

A true shepherd knows his sheep, and they know him. There is a trust that is developed between the sheep and the shepherd. This is what David spoke about in Psalm 23, known as the Shepherd's Psalm. "(A Psalm of David.) The LORD is my shepherd; I shall not want. He maketh me to lie down in green pastures: he leadeth me beside the still waters. He restoreth my soul: he leadeth me in the paths of righteousness for his name's sake. Yea, though I walk through the valley of the shadow of death, I will fear no evil: for thou art with me; thy rod and thy staff they comfort me. Thou preparest a table before me in the presence of mine enemies: thou anointest my head with oil; my cup runneth over. Surely goodness and mercy shall follow me all the days of my life: and I will dwell in the house of the LORD for ever."

This psalm speaks of comfort and security from the perspective of a sheep who is known and loved by their shepherd. Jesus refers to Himself as the "Good Shepherd" who "giveth his life for the sheep." (John 10:11)

The word *pastor* is found only one time in the New Testament in Ephesians 4:11 where the Greek word is *poimen*. It is used here in the context of the five-fold ministry gifts which God has given to His church. Along with the gifts of apostles, prophets, evangelists, and teachers, the gift of the pastor has been given that the church may be perfected or completed in order to do the work of the ministry. The idea is that these ministers would develop the individuals under their care bringing them to spiritual maturity. This is what discipleship is. The mature disciple will, in turn, make other disciples, and the church will be edified, or built up. That is the biblical paradigm for church growth.

In every other occurrence of the use of this word in the New Testament, it is translated *shepherd*. Jesus often used the words *shepherd and sheep* to express His relationship to the people. Jesus made it very clear in His analogy of the sheep to shepherd relationship. The shepherd is going to be intimately aware of each of his sheep and know what each one needs.

Many large churches do a very fine job at assuring that the sheep are well cared for. They have a structure in place where there is sufficient accountability through assistant pastors, group leaders, affinity groups, and the like. But there is a danger intrinsic to the modern Church Growth Movement. Many sheep get lost in the fold.

I am intimately aware of a family who left a small church to attend a larger church. The pastor of the small church had been instrumental in leading several members of that family to Christ. He spent countless hours in counsel helping them through many difficult situations. He wept with them in their trials and rejoiced with them in their victories. Apparently, they felt as a family that they were missing something, and so they moved on. They had been attending the large church for approximately a year and a half when the pastors of the two churches had the opportunity to meet. The names of the family members were mentioned by the small church pastor, and the pastor of the large church had no idea who they were.

I am aware of another occasion where a family left a small church to attend a large church. This family found themselves in a crisis where they needed pastoral counsel, yet they didn't feel as though they could call upon the large church pastor.

I do not cite these issues simply to be critical, but to make an important point. As it has been said for many years, the grass is not always greener on the other side of the fence. The very definition of the word *pastor* implies an intimate relationship with the sheep of the fold.

There used to be what might be considered a common courtesy. I would argue it is a biblical responsibility. When people would show up at another church, the pastor would do what he could to restore the people to their fellowship. People come and go so often these days. But if someone returns for a few weeks, it is generally a good idea to know something about them. First of all, it is important to know who is coming into the fold. As a shepherd, you need to know for the sake of protecting the flock. I want to know who is coming into the fold and why. I want to know what they believe; if they are teachable; and what are their intentions. Jude addressed this in his epistle (Jude 4).

Very often people leave a church over a disagreement or a misunderstanding. Just because someone shows up at your door doesn't mean they are your sheep. After a couple of weeks of attendance, I believe a conversation is in order. We should offer to help restore people to their fellowship if at all possible. I believe this is our responsibility as shepherds. I know I would appreciate if a pastor attempted to restore a disgruntled sheep from this fold. I fear this courtesy has been long forgotten. It seems to be every man for himself, and I believe this grieves the Good Shepherd, whose sheep they really are.

There is a lot to be learned from the interaction between Jesus and Peter at the seashore after the Resurrection (John 21:15-17). I will address the part that relates to shepherding here and address the responsibility aspect in the next chapter.

Most English translations use the word "feed" in all three statements of Jesus in this text. The original Greek text is different. In verse 15, Jesus tells Peter to "Feed My lambs." The lambs are the little ones, or young sheep. These could be likened to new believers in Christ. They are lambs. Their needs are different than those of the rest of the flock. They must not be left to wander and fend for themselves. Great care must be given to them if they are to grow and mature properly.

When the apostle Paul wrote to the Corinthian church, he told them that they were not ready for "Spiritual food." He told them that he had to feed them with milk and not with meat because they couldn't handle the meat of the word. The leaders of the church at Corinth were allowing those who were professing a conversion experience to join their ranks without forsaking their sinful lives. Until they were willing to turn away from worldliness, they were not ready to mature (I Corinthians 3:1-3). As shepherds, we must make sure those attending our churches understand completely what it means to "come to Christ." Everyone professing faith in Christ must come out of the world and separate themselves to the Lord. They are to leave their sinful lifestyle behind ("the unclean thing") and follow the Lord in righteousness (II Corinthians 6:17). When pastors baptize new believers who are knowingly cohabitating, they are not properly caring for Jesus' lambs. This is one of the more obvious and, unfortunately, more frequent examples of sinful lifestyles not being forsaken. But the list is sadly a long one. Pastors should be more concerned with the *quality* and not the *quantity* of the flock entrusted to them.

Jesus then said, *"Shepherd* My sheep." These would be the mature sheep. They need to be shepherded. We must not assume because they have been on their Christian journey for any length of time that they do not need a shepherd. Paul referred to this as "perfecting the saints for the work of the ministry" (Ephesians 4:11-12). There has been a misunderstanding in the Christian church for many years. It is due in part to a misapplied comma in the older King James Bibles (in some of the newer printings of the KJV this has been corrected). It is known as the "deadly comma." In verse 12 the commas sort of create a list of responsibilities for the five-fold ministry gifts. "For the perfecting of the saints, for the work of the ministry, for the edifying of the body of Christ." Reading it this way, it would appear that it is the pastor's job to do the work of the ministry. Paul's intention was that we would perfect, or complete the saints resulting in the saints doing the work of the ministry. The pastor's job is to assist each individual under his or her care in identifying their ministry gifts and utilizing them in the furtherance of the Kingdom of God. Some will minister within the church, others will minister outside of the church, but all are to be involved in some sort of ministry. Sheep beget sheep. And they all need a shepherd to guide them in their maturing.

Next, Jesus said, "Feed My sheep." Yes, the sheep still need to be fed. The writer of Hebrews said, "But strong meat belongeth to them that are of full age, even those who by reason of use have their senses exercised to discern both good and evil." (Hebrews 5:12). Paul in his writing to the Colossian church prays for their maturity. "For this cause we also, since the day we heard it, do not cease to pray for you, and to desire that ye might be filled with the knowledge of His will in all wisdom and spiritual understanding; that ye might walk worthy of the Lord unto all pleasing, being fruitful in every good work, and increasing in the knowledge of God." (Colossians 1:9-10). No matter how old, or how long one has been walking with the Lord, every believer should continue to grow in the knowledge of God. God is infinite; therefore, it will take all eternity to discover all there is to know of Him. Paul himself was committed to continual personal spiritual growth (Philippians 3:12-14). Pastors must make sure their sheep are being fed regardless of their tenure.

Sheep are some of the most helpless creatures on earth. They don't have fangs, claws, antlers, venom, shells, or any other means of defense. It is not that they are not intelligent, but when they get in trouble, there is very little they could do to get themselves out. If the shepherd is not acutely aware of the wellbeing of each lamb or sheep, they could be lost. Jesus said a good shepherd will do what is necessary to restore one lost sheep even if he has 100 sheep (Matthew 18:12). He cannot leave it up to those who are hired to assist him (John 10:12-13). That is not to say that assistant pastors are hirelings. That is not at all what I am intending to imply. But the biblical example of a shepherd is of one who knows each little lamb and every mature sheep in his fold. There comes a point in the numerical growth of a church where this is practically impossible.

Our Responsibility

As I said in the last chapter, there is a responsibility aspect in the context of the discourse between Jesus and Peter found in John 21:15-17. First, let us look at why Peter was out fishing in the first place. Some say it was because he and the other disciples didn't know what to do after the Resurrection. Jesus had not yet told them to wait in Jerusalem. That is possible. But I believe Peter was quitting. He had denied Jesus just as Jesus said he would. Jesus was leaving and the dreams of following the King in His new Kingdom were gone. Nothing was turning out the way he had thought. What Peter knew was fishing. That's where he was when Jesus found him, that is where he was going back. "I know how to fish. I'm going back to fishing." But Jesus had other plans.

This is how I see it. Peter had a commitment problem. He had no problem voicing his commitment, he just had a problem with the follow-through. "Though all men shall be offended because of thee, yet will I never be offended... Though I should die with thee, yet will I not deny thee. Likewise also said all the disciples." (Matthew 26:33, 35). That same night, on three occasions he denied he knew Jesus. "And Peter remembered the words of Jesus and he went out, and wept bitterly." (V.75). He thought himself an utter failure.

Now at the water's edge, Jesus is restoring Peter. He had told Peter that he would fail. "And the Lord said, 'Simon, Simon, behold, Satan hath desired to have you, that he may sift you as wheat: But I have prayed for thee, that thy faith fail not: and when thou art converted, strengthen thy brethren." (Luke 22:31-32).

Failing isn't falling down. Failing is not getting back up when you are given the chance. There are many times along this journey when I have felt like a failure. I'm sure you have, too. Especially when you see other churches growing, and yours isn't.

I believe there is a hunger deep within the heart of those who have been awakened by the Holy Spirit. The superficial sermons that are often being preached in the modern church will not satisfy that deep hunger. There will come a time I believe in the near future where those hungry for more of God will be led to pastors and teachers who continue to rightly divide the Word of truth. Where pastors are bringing forth the milk, the bread, and the meat of God's Word there will be church growth. When difficult times come to our nation, and they will, superficial sermons will not be enough for those longing for spiritual shelter. God will send the spiritually hungry to where the spiritual food is being served. This I believe with all my heart.

Jesus asked Peter three times if Peter loved Him (John 21:15-17). But the words He used are not interchangeable. In verse 15, Jesus used the word agape. Agape has the meaning of intense, absolute, sacrificial love. "Peter, do you love Me like that?" Peter answered, "Lord, Thou knowest that I love You." The word he used was phileo, meaning friendship, or brotherly love. "Lord, you know I have *that* kind of love for You." Again Jesus asked Peter if he loved Him with agape love. Peter again answered that he loved Him with phileo love. The third time Jesus asked him if he loved Him with phileo love. This is what upset Peter. Not that He asked him the third time, but the way in which He asked. Jesus was asking Peter for the commitment He had voiced in the past. Peter could not commit. All he could commit to was friendship. Jesus then asked Peter if he could even commit to friendship. This was the best Peter had. In light of his recent denials, and his return to his old business, he was afraid to make a commitment he could not keep.

Peter expresses his concern about another of Jesus' disciples. "Lord, and what shall this man do?" (V.21). Jesus said, in essence, "Don't worry about anyone else.

Just take care of your own issues and follow Me." (V.22).

We get so concerned with what others are doing. I see things that some of my peers are doing in their ministries and I rejoice with them that they are seeing fruit. I see other things that others are doing, and I do not agree. But in neither case is it my business. My responsibility is to follow Jesus in what He is leading me to do. I am only responsible for my own corner of the vineyard.

Our responsibility is first to the Lord. Speaking through the prophet Ezekiel, the Lord warned the watchmen of Israel (Ezekiel 33). If they were aware of the danger and warned the people, the responsibility for their deliverance would rest with the people. If the people hearkened to the warning they would live. If they did not hearken, they would die, but the watchman would be free of the responsibility. But if the watchman failed to warn the people, and anyone was destroyed, "his blood will I require at the watchman's hand." (V.6)

He went on to say to the watchmen, "When I say unto the wicked, 'O wicked man, thou shalt surely die;' if thou dost not speak to warn the wicked from his way, that wicked man shall die in his iniquity; but his blood will I require at thine hand." (V.8) My friend, I believe it is far more important to fashion one's ministry after the mandate God has put forth in His Word than to fashion it after a desire to grow one's church. I believe this is what Jude had in mind when he wrote his epistle. He said, "Beloved, when I gave all diligence to write unto you of the common salvation, it was needful for me to write unto you, and exhort you that ye should earnestly contend for the faith which was once delivered unto the saints." (V.3) His initial intention appears to be to share about the joy he and his audience had in common regarding their salvation. He wanted to celebrate. And there are certainly great times of celebration. But Jude said it was important to urge them to contend for the faith or, fight for the truth. The greatest need the lost world has is to hear a clear presentation of the gospel of Jesus Christ. A call to repentance. Celebration follows repentance. It doesn't replace it. Jesus said the angels rejoice when one sinner repents (Luke 15:10)

As pastors, our greatest responsibility to God is to rescue the perishing. He has charged us with this task. When we stand before Him, I do not believe He will be concerned with the number of members in our churches. He will hold us accountable for the stewardship of the gospel of the kingdom.

The passage of Scripture that shakes me to the very core of my being is Matthew 7:21-23. "Not every one that saith unto me, Lord, Lord, shall enter into the kingdom of heaven; but he that doeth the will of my Father which is in heaven. And then will I profess unto them, I never knew you: depart from me, ye that work iniquity." Jesus emphatically states that there will be "many" in the church who will minister in His name and believe they are His servants, yet in reality, He never knew them. To be successful according to the standard God has established, ministers should be more concerned with their commitment to the Scriptures than to their own personal assessment of success based upon their ability to draw a crowd. Being faithful in preaching the gospel will result in hearing, "Well done, good and faithful servant: thou hast been faithful over a few things. I will make thee ruler over many things: enter thou into the joy of thy Lord." (Matthew 25:23).

What has the Lord called you to do? I'm amazed at some of the changes being made in the modern church in order to draw crowds. In many cases, it is nothing short of compromise.

As I had said in the beginning of this book, when I was first saved the Lord led me to a wonderful church to sit under the ministry of a great pastor. It was that pastor who first recognized God's call on my life. He helped me to identify the call and assisted me in developing my ministry. The most important thing I gleaned from his example was to stand upon solid principles. I drew an "X" in my mind and in my heart.

This is where I'll stand. There would be forces at work against me to try to move me from my position, but I would continue to stand on the "X." Others would change their positions, even compromising their once held beliefs, but I would not compromise. Not that I would ever compare myself to Martin Luther, but I sometimes feel like echoing his words. "Here I stand, I can do no other, so help me God. Amen."

I grew up hearing, "Don't just stand there, do something!" (Usually when I was in trouble for not lending a helping hand around the house). Unfortunately, this is what we do. When things aren't going the way we want them to, we feel we need to *do something*. If the church we are pastoring isn't growing, we think we better do something. No. Don't just do something, stand there! Stand where God has called you to stand.

We are responsible to the believers under our pastoral care. As previously stated, we are to perfect the saints for the work of the ministry. We are to feed, nurture, and guide the sheep. Make sure what you are serving is spiritually nutritious.

When our children were growing up there was always a healthy meal on the table. My wife made sure of it. There were times when we called our children to the table, and they didn't come. At least, not right away. Why wouldn't they come when there was such good food prepared for them? Perhaps they were playing games or with their toys and were too busy to eat. They were hungry, but they were having too much fun. Another reason they might not have come to the table is that they had been eating junk food. Empty calories. It tasted good, but there was little to no nutritional value. They weren't hungry anymore, but they were not healthy, either. Or they didn't come because they didn't like what was being served. Spinach, broccoli, peas… liver. They didn't care that it was healthy, it didn't taste good. There is one more possibility, and it must not be overlooked. It could be possible that they had an eating disorder. They could have been starving to death but didn't realize it. They thought they were fat, but they were actually undernourished.

We could have changed the menu and given them the sweets they wanted. We could have changed the way we served dinner, sitting in front of the TV as they ate. Or we could provide the best meal we could possibly prepare and expect them to come to dinner. As parents, our responsibility to our children was not dictated by their desires. It was determined by what we knew was best for them.

We also have a responsibility to the lost. We are to rescue the perishing. A watered-down sermon without the conviction of the gospel will not help anyone. It may cause the church to grow, but to what end? Do we love them enough to tell them the truth? Do we love the Lord enough to obey Him?   "And that repentance and remission of sins should be preached in His name among all nations, beginning at Jerusalem." (Luke 24:47). We must preach repentance. Otherwise, we are doing more harm than good. If we invite people to our church services and only tell them of the love of God without warning them of the judgment to come, we are giving them a false sense of security. They will not seek to be saved if they think they already are. They must hear the whole counsel of God.

Moving the Boundaries

There is a road in my hometown leading to the airport. When we were children, my parents would take my siblings and me to park at the airport and watch the airplanes take off and land. It was a small airport, mostly for private planes with one or two small commercial outfits. There wasn't very much on the road in the way of industry. An ice cream shop, a small factory, and a few other small businesses along the way. For the most part, it was a fairly quiet road. There was one lane running east and one lane running west.

Over the years the airport began to grow offering additional commercial flights. A hotel was built on that road to accommodate the travelers using the airport. Several small factories were built, a couple of overnight shipping companies moved in followed by several fast food restaurants. Traffic became a problem, so the town officials put a plan in place to widen the road. Traffic was diverted for a season while they brought in the heavy equipment, and the process began.

The first step was demolition. The old curbs needed to be bulldozed, as well as the sidewalks. The grass along the edge was dug up, and the telephone poles were moved back maybe twenty feet, and all the wires restrung. The old road was gone. In some stretches along the road, an additional lane was made in both directions. In other parts of the road, there were two lanes added in each direction to accommodate the increasing traffic. New sidewalks were poured, new grass was planted, new road signs were placed along the edge, and the project was completed.

I remember how that road used to be. Granted, change was necessary. But I couldn't tell you *exactly* where the old road was; *exactly* where the boundaries were. They are gone forever. Anyone going down that road now for the first time would have no way of knowing what the road used to be like, or where the curbs or sidewalks, or telephone poles once stood.

That road, ironically enough named Lordship Boulevard, was once a narrow road. Now it is a broad way. I see a similar thing taking place in the Church Growth Movement. The once narrow road is being widened.

Jesus said, "Enter ye in at the strait gate: for wide is the gate, and broad is the way, that leadeth to destruction, and many there be which go thereat:

Because strait is the gate, and narrow is the way, which leadeth unto life, and few there be that find it." (Matthew 7:13-14). His very next statement is, "Beware of false prophets, which come to you in sheep's clothing, but inwardly they are ravening wolves." (V.15). Luke recorded Jesus as saying, "Strive to enter in at the strait gate: for many, I say unto you, will seek to enter in, and shall not be able." (Luke 13:24). *To strive* in the Greek text is defined as "To engage in an athletic contest, to fight, to struggle, to strive." It is the word from which we get our word *agony*. Jesus was not inferring from this text that we must work our way into heaven. He was indicating the effort that would be required to stay on the strait and narrow road. He was warning of the many false prophets who would come and teach a false gospel that would lead many astray.

In a different context, Jesus expressed the effort needed to enter the Kingdom of God. "And from the days of John the Baptist until now the kingdom of heaven suffereth violence, and the violent take it by force." (Matthew 11:12). This does not mean there would need to be a violent uprising or hostile takeover. What it means is that the Kingdom is taken hold of only by forceful people who are committed to breaking away from the world and turning to Christ no matter what the cost.

Nearly two thousand years ago Jesus said the road that leads to salvation was a narrow road. Two thousand years later that road is still narrow.

I've watched as changes have taken place in the church world. Just as the heavy equipment was brought in to move the curbs and the sidewalks, teachers have come into the church and moved the boundaries. Those who once walked "the strait and narrow" recognize the difference. The problem is that it is now difficult to tell where the boundaries used to be. Those boundaries are being moved inch by inch. How long before the church in America becomes the broad way? Are we at that point now?

The Barna Group recently released the results of a study that shows 47% of Christian Millennials believe evangelizing is wrong[2]. The acceptance of homosexuality and the cohabitation of heterosexual couples is growing in the Christian church world. Abortion is becoming an acceptable form of birth control. The use of alcohol, or what we used to call "sipping saints" is on the rise. I do not here intend to create a list of sins. I only mention these as a sample of the many things that are now acceptable for Christians to do, which Scripture directly condemns. Many pastors won't address any of these issues for fear of offending someone and having them leave their church.

I'm not talking about being rude or obnoxious. I'm

not talking about needlessly offending people with "turn or burn" statements. I'm talking about speaking the truth in love. Many were offended by Jesus, "And they were offended in him. But Jesus said unto them, "A prophet is not without honour, save in his own country, and in his own house." (Matthew 13:57). The Son of God who came to express the love of God (John 3:16) was an offense to many. Who were those offended? Proud sinners, religious leaders, those who would not repent of their sins and follow Jesus.

The word *offense* in these passages means a "stumbling block" in the way. They disapproved of what He had to tell them. But Jesus didn't change His message. He continued to call the world to repentance.

A generation has arisen that has said, "We will not have this message." Paul warned us of such a day. He said, "The time will come when they will not endure sound doctrine; but after their own lusts shall they heap to themselves teachers, having itching ears." (II Timothy 4:3). The word *lusts* in this context does not necessarily mean sexual desires, but all desires of the flesh. They want comfort and encouragement. There is a great need for comfort and encouragement in this world, and God's word will certainly do that. But only hearing words of comfort is like a steady diet of junk food; it tastes great but with no nutritional value.

The Church Growth Movement has said in essence,

"Well, if you will not have this message, what message *will* you have? We will give you *that*." Jesus never asked the multitudes what they wanted to hear. He spoke only that which the Father sent Him to speak.

The apostle Paul didn't survey the neighborhood to determine what they wanted to hear. He said, "But we preach Christ crucified, unto the Jews a stumblingblock, and unto the Greeks foolishness; But unto them which are called, both Jews and Greeks, Christ the power of God, and the wisdom of God." (I Corinthians 1:23-24). The preaching of the Cross was not *popular*. In light of what Jesus said about the broad way, when something becomes popular, it ought to send up a red flag. Paul said, "I am crucified with Christ..." (Galatians 2:20). He said, "I die daily." (I Corinthians 15:31). He said, "But God forbid that I should glory, save in the cross of our Lord Jesus Christ, by whom the world is crucified unto me, and I unto the world." (Galatians 6:14). As a result, Paul could say, "Henceforth there is laid up for me a crown of righteousness, which the Lord, the righteous judge, shall give me at that day: and not to me only, but unto all them also that love his appearing." (II Timothy 4:8). This is not popular preaching. So many pastors no longer preach the Cross. What has become popular is a crown without a cross. Or as what someone coined "easy believeism."

The gospel is an offense to those who are living outside of the Righteousness of the kingdom of God. Jesus, the gospel personified, came that He might be a stumbling block. He is referred to in both Testaments as "a stone of stumbling and rock of offense" (Isaiah 8:14; I Peter 2:8). Jesus said, "And whosoever shall fall on this stone shall be broken but on whomsoever it shall fall, it will grind him to powder." (Matthew 21:44). The gospel is the good news of Jesus Christ and His gift of salvation. He stands in our path to confront us with our sin. He says in essence, "You will go to hell *over My dead Body*." Those who fall upon Him in repentance will be broken. Broken in the sense of a contrite heart and a broken spirit. He will be to them a sanctuary; a place of refuge (Isaiah 8:14). But those who will not fall upon Him, He will one day *fall upon* in judgment, and they will *be ground to powder*.

Pastors who are afraid to offend in fear of losing numbers are not expressing the love of God. If I knew a person had a deadly disease and I knew where they could receive the antidote for free, what would you think of me if I remained quiet for fear of offending them? You wouldn't think of me as very loving at all. In fact, I could rightfully be accused of being unloving and evil.

Before dawn on June 28, 1983, in Greenwich, Connecticut a one-hundred-foot section of I-95 known as the Mianus River Bridge collapsed killing three people. Witnesses said the vehicles "just seemed to disappear." One unnamed hero stood in the middle of the highway in the darkness and waved oncoming traffic to a halt. Had he not been there, or had he not risked his life standing in the middle of the highway in the darkness, there is no doubt many more would have perished.

This is what a pastor does. They get out in the middle of the broad way warning of the dangers ahead. If anyone has not confessed their sin before God and repented of those sins acknowledging the vicarious death of Jesus Christ, for them the bridge is out.

I return to the topic of moving boundaries. Proverbs 22:28 asserts that we "Remove not the ancient landmark, which thy fathers have set." Landmarks were often stone pillars placed in the corners of properties. In New England, you can hardly walk through the woods without coming upon a stone wall. In early America, properties were designated by stone walls. Today most properties are marked with metal pins buried just below the surface. If there is ever a property dispute, these pins are easily found with a metal detector and pegged above ground with stakes.

The church property where I now pastor was once encroached upon. Our neighbors to the north put up a rose trellis and planted flowers and shrubs on our property. They cut down a tree which was clearly not theirs. They were enjoying about fifteen feet of land that did not belong to them. Being the good neighbors that we are, we pointed out the error and offered to allow them the continued use of the property they had claimed as long as they understood that it did, in fact, belong to the church. All was fine until they put their home up for sale. They were presenting the parcel as a part of the property they were selling. It was necessary to contract a surveyor who located the property markers and placed the appropriate flags on the corners of the property. Had we not acted, the land could have been lost to us forever.

This proverb originated in the Old Testament law regarding ownership of properties and the handing down of those properties to the proper heirs. Deuteronomy 19:14 states, "Thou shalt not remove thy neighbor's landmark, which thou shalt inherit in the land that the Lord thy God giveth thee to possess it." It was against the law to move the established boundaries designating property ownership. This law became a proverb and was later used in spiritual matters. Hosea addresses the leaders of Judah who were no longer walking in obedience to the Lord. "The princes of Judah were like them that remove the bound: therefore, I will pour out my wrath upon them like water." (Hosea 5:10).

The Boundaries are being moved. Many of the things that are promoted in the modern church to attract attendance today would never have been allowed even thirty years ago. I feel like we are on the Starship Enterprise, "boldly going where no man has gone before." In fact, many of the things being promoted by church leaders today would have put my credentials in jeopardy had I attempted to allow them in the past. What was wrong then is wrong now. What was sin then is sin now. The gate is still strait. The way is still narrow.

I hear pastors talking about the "new thing" God is doing in their churches. They use this phrase almost as if it gives them the liberty to do anything they want. The inference is that what was old is no longer valid. First, it is often taken out of context. Isaiah spoke of the new thing God would do. (Isaiah 43:19). It's amazing the things God gets blamed for under the banner of God's *new thing*. In context, Isaiah was prophesying a time for Israel when God would deliver them from Babylonian captivity; a captivity brought about as punishment for Israel's disobedience. The new thing God would do was restoration and a new beginning for them. God was calling His people back to the old ways; the ways of obedience.

Worship in Spirit and Truth

One of the most important aspects of church life is worship. In fact, worship is a very important part of all Christian life. When Jesus encountered the Samaritan woman at the well, He had a conversation with her regarding worship. He said, "But the hour cometh, and now is, when the true worshippers shall worship the Father in spirit and in truth: for the Father seeketh such to worship him. God is a Spirit: and they that worship him must worship him in spirit and in truth." (John 4:23-24). The Father is seeking, desiring those who will worship Him properly. When I say properly, I do not mean to say that there is a legalistic approach to worship. But we clearly see throughout Scripture that there is true worship and false worship.

God had instructed Moses to burn incense to Him as an expression of worship. Nadab and Abihu, the sons of Aaron, offered incense which was burning on firepans of strange fire. (Leviticus 10:1-2). It seemed to be acceptable to them in that it was incense and it was fire. However, the only acceptable fire was the fire of the holy altar. That fire that was to burn perpetually had been started by God Himself. It was the fire of the Spirit. The fire of God had come down from heaven and consumed the sacrifice on the altar (Leviticus 9:24). It was only that fire that was acceptable for the burning of incense because it originated with God. Because they offered fire that originated with themselves and not with God, a fire came out from the presence of God and consumed them both. Not all "worship" is acceptable to God.

I must confess I do not understand this trend in the modern church world. Everyone is turning down the house lights, projecting blue lights on the altar, and plugging in smoke machines. There is an attempt to create an environment or atmosphere of praise and worship. I guess the idea is that if the proper environment is created, then God will come down and receive the praise and worship of the people. If there was a power failure, they wouldn't know what to do. I believe this is a mockery of the glory of God. It is a cheap imitation of what God is seeking from His people. In Exodus chapter 40, God instructed Moses to set up the tabernacle in the wilderness. Moses did as the Lord instructed. "Then a cloud covered the tent of the congregation, and the glory of the Lord filled the tabernacle." (V.34). This glory is what rabbis later referred to as the "shekinah" glory of God which is a

Hebrew word meaning "dwelling of God." We see it again in Solomon's temple when he dedicated the temple to the Lord. The glory of the Lord filled the temple with a cloud of smoke (I Kings 8:11). In the future Tribulation in "the temple of the tabernacle of the testimony in heaven" the "temple was filled with smoke from the glory of God, and from His power" (Revelation 15:5, 8). As I see it, when the Lord shows up, *He brings His own smoke*. He doesn't need us to try to manufacture His presence.

The focus has turned to the quality and experience of worship rather than the content of the music and intention of the heart. Many churches advertise how good their worship experience is. There is an attempt to put together the best praise and worship band. I hear people grading the worship at various churches. The statements express how they feel. If they felt good the worship was good. If they didn't feel good, the worship was not good. God never once told us to measure the quality of worship by how we feel. True worship has nothing at all to do with how we feel. It is not man-ward but Godward. "Good" worship is worship that is solely for the glory and honor of God. It is wonderful if it is given by experienced musicians with a professional quality sound. It is equally wonderful when it is given without any instruments at all. I love beautiful music. I long for a full orchestra and large choir to lift praise and worship to our glorious Lord who deserves our very best. But in the absence of such, we could still glorify God with whatever we have available. In many small churches there are few or no musicians. We use split tracks in our worship services. The best part about using tracks is that the "musicians" always show up for church and on time. We pray about the songs we sing, and we sing with all our hearts to the glory of God.

Having said what I did about our feelings, let me add this. There are times in the worship of our Lord that we will *feel* His presence. Personally, there are times when His presence is so real in our worship that I weep with joy. The goal, however, is not our feelings. The goal is glorifying God. But God, being the giving Father that He is will bless us with the feeling of His presence. I explain it this way. When I was young and would visit my grandfather, I never left his house without him giving me a little gift. Sometimes it was a quarter; sometimes a little toy, but it was always something. I didn't go to my grandfather's house to get the gift. I went to his house to visit him. I loved my grandfather, and I loved to be with him. But my grandfather loved me, too, and always wanted to bless me when I was with him. What would have happened if I started looking for the gift? "Hey Gramps, where's my prize?" It would have utterly destroyed our relationship. Rather than going to his house to express my love for him, I would have become a selfish taker. I believe when we come into the presence of God with the primary expectation of feeling good, we are not worshipping Him in spirit or in truth.

I said I would love to have an orchestra in our church to worship God. Until the Lord sends us one or raises one up from within our fellowship, we will do the best we can with what we have. But there is another trend in the modern church. In an attempt to create "good worship," pastors are hiring musicians to play the music during a worship service. I'm not talking about paid music staff in the church. What I am referring to is the practice of hiring unbelievers on the worship team because they are good musicians or have good voices. It is impossible to worship a God one does not know. Unless a person has been born again by the Spirit of God, their worship cannot be in Spirit or in truth. It is like Nadab and Abihu offering strange fire. It does not originate with God and is therefore not acceptable to Him.

There is a model in the Old Testament for worship seen in the temple in Jerusalem. In simple terms, it was made up of three areas: the outer court, also known as the Court of the Gentiles, the inner court, and the Most Holy place, or Holy of Holies. The outer court was open to all. Gentiles were free to enter the outer court.

Taking this as our example, all are welcome in our church. Unbelievers are invited and welcome. In fact, we pray they will show up. Our hope is that they will hear the Word of God, repent of their sins and be born again by the Spirit of God. They are welcome to sing along with us as we praise our God. When the church sings the songs of praise, the unbeliever is somewhat left behind. They could acknowledge what God has done, but not from a heart of faith. But when it comes to the songs of worship, they cannot enter. To be sure they are welcome to sing the songs, but they cannot worship in Spirit and in truth. To sing songs of adoration which express a love for God one must know God and love Him. Unless a person has been regenerated by God's Holy Spirit, their worship is as the incense of Nadab and Abihu.

The purpose of a worship team is to lead the congregation in worship to our God. Unfortunately, in many churches, the worship service has become a spectator event. The worship team performs the music as the congregation watches. In order to lead someone somewhere, the leader would need to know the way. The unsaved, unregenerate musician or singer cannot possibly lead the congregation into the presence of the Lord having never been there themselves.

In our example in the temple, the Holy of Holies was entered only by the High Priest, and that not without the sprinkling of the blood of the atonement. Jesus is our High Priest who has entered into the Most Holy place with the sprinkling of His own Blood. He has called us to the priesthood of the believer (I Peter 2:5) where we could now enter before the throne of Grace.

About music in the church, I believe there is still a place for the old hymns. I love many of the modern praise and worship choruses and look forward to more being written. Many of the hymns of bygone days were written out of deep love for God. They became a part of the history of the Christian Church offering a sense of heritage and stability. If there is one thing lacking in our modern society it is stability. We live in an ever-changing world. I see a tremendous increase in anxiety in people I counsel today. Very often the anxiety comes from a sense of instability. People are desperate for something of substance to hold on to. The old hymns of the church might offer them something of heritage reminding them that they belong to something ageless. Also, the content of the old hymns is something to note. Many of the hymns of the church are Scripture put to music. It was a way of making God's Word easier to memorize. It's good to have a balance of the old and the new. I know some of our older members certainly appreciate the place of honor we give to the hymns.

Jesus said the Father is seeking those who will worship Him in spirit and in truth.

Leadership Everything

Have you noticed how often the topic of leadership comes up in the Church Growth Movement? Years ago, pastors were simply called *pastors*, or if they led a church staff, they were referred to as *Senior Pastors*. Now they are called *lead pastors* emphasizing their leadership. Many of the books and seminars on church growth center on the topic of leadership. The assertion is that in order to have a growing church you must have properly trained leadership. I would agree there are advantages to having leaders who could lead, but the emphasis is misplaced. When Jesus prepared His disciples to lead His church after His departure to heaven, He taught them by example. Notice what He said about leadership and the exercising of authority. "But Jesus called them to Him, and saith unto them, 'Ye know that they which are accounted to rule over the Gentiles exercise lordship over them; and their great ones exercise authority upon them. But so shall it not be among you: but whosoever will be great among you, shall be your minister: And whosoever of you will be chiefest, shall be servant of all. For even the Son of man came not to be ministered unto, but to minister, and to give His life a ransom for many." (Mark 10:42-45). The word for *minister* here is the word from which we get our word *deacon,* meaning "one who serves." The one who will be the chief or *leader* will be the servant (slave) of all. Jesus was making the point that in the secular world, leadership is expressed with authority being exercised over one another, whereas in the governance of the church, leadership would be expressed through servanthood. Jesus referred to His own life as a *ransom*; a price paid to obtain the freedom of others. We understand this in His vicarious death on the Cross for the salvation of mankind. But He is stating this ransom as the standard of servanthood that His disciples were to adopt. If anyone wants to be a leader in His church, it will not be by their organizational skills or their brainstorming sessions. It will not be by their ability to understand demographics and apply principles of leadership to their target group. It will not be by leadership skills learned in a conference. Funny, I have never seen an advertisement for a *Servant and Slave* conference. Yet this is exactly the attitude Jesus taught that His disciples must have if they were to properly lead His church.

One of the last things Jesus did with His disciples the last night He was with them was to wash their feet.

Generally when a person is departing, their last words and actions hold the greatest measure of weight and impact. The last thing said is often the most important thing to remember. Jesus washed their feet. "If I then, your Lord and Master, have washed your feet, ye also ought to wash one another's feet. For I have given you an example, that ye should do as I have done." (John 13:13-14).

The example is in the principle and not necessarily in the exact action itself. I know there are church fellowships that practice foot washing as one of their church ordinances. I am not speaking against the practice. I am told by many that it is a very humbling experience, both for the one doing the washing and for the one whose feet are being washed.

In the eastern world especially in biblical times, foot washing was a regularly practiced custom. Open sandals were the common footwear, and with the dusty roads, feet would become quite dirty. It was customary for the servant in a home to wash the feet of the household and any guests that might come calling. Jesus, the Teacher, the Leader took His place on His knees before His own disciples as a servant to them all. He set the example of what true leadership should be. It would be through servanthood.

There are many things a pastor could do in the execution of their pastoral duties to minister to their people. Obviously, Spirit-led biblical preaching and doctrinal teaching are on the list. Lifting their parishioners in prayer on a regular basis and in times of distress is certainly a part. But these and many other tasks can be performed from a distance. In Christ's example to His disciples in the washing of their feet, we find an intimacy that cannot be achieved from afar. There is a personal touch necessary in the carrying out of this activity. Whether a person believes in the practice of actually washing one another's feet as an ordinance of the church, or whether they see in this only an example of servanthood matters little. The point Jesus is clearly making is that to be a leader of His people, one needs to be a humble servant to those people, and to do so one needs to be personally involved.

What might a practical application of this principle be within a modern western culture? If foot washing was the work of a servant, and a menial task, the pastor should be willing and available to assist church members or anyone at all for that matter in any way necessary. In simpler terms, there should be no class distinction between the leadership of a church and its membership. We are all servants of one another.

The idea of an entourage escorting the pastor to and from the podium so as not to have personal contact with the membership is a foreign concept to the teaching of Jesus, and later Paul, I might add.

I understand the concept of authority in church government. I appreciate the respect the office of the pastor is given. It appears to be by divine will and appointment that there are leaders placed in each church. (Acts 14:13; 20:17; Philippians 1:1; James 5:14). These leaders are called elders, bishops, overseers, or pastors. The purpose appears to be the stewardship of the church. The apostle Paul outlined the requirements of his leadership position when writing to both Timothy and Titus (I Timothy 3:1-7; Titus 1:6-9). But leadership in Christ's church is not to be exercised by authority over, but service to His people.

Making the Man

In a townhall meeting at Camp Buering in Kuwait on December 8, 2004, Army Specialist Thomas Wilson asked Secretary of Defense Donald Rumsfeld a question regarding the lack of proper protective shielding on the military vehicles. Secretary Rumsfeld responded saying, "As you know, ah, you go to war with the army you have – not the army you might want or wish to have at a later time." I won't get into the context or the politics of his answer. I only mention this dialogue because that statement has stuck with me ever since I heard him say this. "You go to war with the army you have – not the army you might want."

There have been many times I have wished I had a bigger "army." Times I wish the church was growing and we had a full complement of staff members. But that isn't the army I have. And there is a battle raging. We have been called into spiritual warfare. There is a very real enemy attempting to destroy us. He has blinded the minds of them who do not believe and holds them in bondage (II Corinthians 4:4). We have been called to set the captive free. The army we have is the army we have, at least for the time being, so we must make the best of what we have.

We may see the army shrink before it grows. I have seen this over the years. It is frightening when you see the numbers diminishing rather than increasing. You may wonder how in the world you are ever going to move the church forward. Imagine how Gideon must have felt. There he was surrounded by the enemy of Midianites. (Judges 6). First of all, he felt inept in his personal abilities. He was the youngest in the house of his father who was least among his own people. The deck was stacked against him from jump street. When God called him to lead Israel against the Midianites, he had an army of 32,000 men (7:3) against an army who were as grasshoppers for multitude (6:5). But according to the Lord, that was too many. God had Gideon give the army a choice to fight or go home. Twenty-two thousand men opted for the latter leaving Gideon only 10,000 men to fight the Midianites. I have felt that same kind of pressure. The enemy lurks all around the church and people continue to leave. Ten thousand men are still too many according to the Lord. The final test was given to see who was really committed to the battle. Only 300 men remained. The Lord had victory in mind for His people. When the victory came, it would be impossible for any man to take credit.

God doesn't need our help. Like Johnathan said to his armor bearer, "There is no restraint to the Lord to save by many or by few." (I Samuel 14:6). When victory comes, it will be solely on the merit of God's grace, and solely for His glory. Until the Lord gives us a bigger army, we must work with the one we have.

When I was in the Army, I was stationed at Ray Barracks, Friedberg, Germany. We were part of the 3rd Armored Division; the "Spearhead" Division. We were guarding the Fulda Gap, the line between East and West Germany. If World War III had broken out, it was believed that this would have been the place it would have begun. The motor pool was full of tanks and trucks, and the armory held all our munitions. It needed to be guarded around the clock. Periodically I would come up on the guard duty roster. Guard duty was an interesting detail. The guard force would show up at Headquarters in the afternoon, and we would be assigned our posts for the next twenty-four hours. It was two hours on duty, and four hours off.

The Guard force was selected from the companies of our battalion; fifteen soldiers in total would show up for inspection. Fifteen men, but only fourteen were required for the detail. The Officer of the Guard would inspect the guard force for readiness. What made guard duty interesting was that there was somewhat of a contest. The man who was most prepared *made the Man* and was given the next twenty-four hours off.

Each of the men on the roster would show up with a fresh shave and haircut. We would starch our fatigues and walk to HQ like wooden soldiers so as not to break the crease in our uniform. Our boots would be highly spit shined, our weapons spotless, our gig lines straight. We would make sure we could recite our General Orders and made ourselves aware of the Orders of the Day. Each man was hoping to make the Man, get a twenty-four-hour pass, change into our "civvies" and catch a train to Frankfurt. Our goal was to get a day off. What was the goal of the Officer of the Guard? Was he just looking to give a guy a day off? No. His goal was to have fourteen men who were well prepared to protect the motor pool.

God is looking for men and women of conviction. Those who will stand to post even when they seem outnumbered. God doesn't count heads, He counts hearts. He told Elijah, He has thousands that have not bowed their knees to Baal. God is looking for men and women of courage.

Before I got to Germany, I was given an all-expense paid trip to Fort Knox, Kentucky by Uncle Sam. This is where I received Basic Training, or *boot camp*. It was there where I learned how to be a soldier. We studied our weapons and how to use them properly to engage our enemy. We learned all we could about the enemy we might face. We learned how to follow orders, and how to carry out our mission. Sometimes the mission was explained to us; sometimes it wasn't. We were learning to follow orders even when they didn't make sense to us. What I learned from my experience is this. All of life is a war. There will be times of rest and relaxation (R&R). There will be twenty-four-hour passes. There will be times when we may get wounded. Sometimes we win the battle, sometimes we lose the battle. But we cannot lose sight of the goal – to win the war. I learned there are two basic types of people: those who are fellow soldiers (they may wear different uniforms), and those who are prisoners of war. Our mission is to assist fellow soldiers along the way and free the prisoners of war. We take our orders from our heavenly Headquarters and stay on the mission until otherwise directed. It might get difficult. People may leave. We may not understand exactly why we are where we are, or what we should do. But until we receive further orders, we are to continue carrying out the last orders we were given.

Basic Training was only eight weeks when I was in the service. That was sufficient for the common soldier. Eight weeks of boot camp, another six to eight weeks of Advanced Individual Training (AIT) where you learned your Military Occupational Skill (MOS), and off to your permanent duty station. But there was another group of soldiers: Special Forces, The Green Berets. Their Basic Training was nine weeks followed by four weeks of AIT, and three weeks of Airborne Training. After that another fourteen to eighteen months of Special Forces Training. These are America's elite. They are the most versatile fighting force on the planet. They have a much greater level of commitment than the common soldier. As the ballad says, "One hundred men will test today, but only three win the Green Beret."

In II Samuel 23, David had his mighty men, or "Mighties." His army consisted of 1.3 million fighting men. Within this group were thirty mighty men. Within this group were *the Three.* Adino, the Tachomite (also known as Jashobeam). He was surrounded by eight hundred enemy troops. He single-handedly slew them all with nothing but a spear. When you have fully committed yourself to the Lord, there is no such thing as outnumbered. Another of the Three was Eleazor, son of Dodo, the Ahohite. He stood alone against the army of the Philistines when the army of Israel retreated. Eleazar stood alone when everyone else fled. His only weapon was a sword. He smote the Philistines until his hand clave to the sword. "And the Lord wrought a great victory that day." (V. 10). Finally

Shammah, the son of Agee, the Hararite. He also stood alone when the rest of the army fled. He stood by himself to defend their land, "And the Lord wrought a great victory." (V.12).

We are all part of the army of God, like the 1.3 million of David's army. But I believe God is calling some to make up His Special Forces.

Repairing the Walls

Hopefully, we have well established the fact that only God could build His church, and we must rely completely upon His Spirit. But we must also be sure we have done all that we could do according to God's direction.

One of the first and most important things I learned in management training is that you can't manage what you can't measure. If our ministry isn't progressing as we might hope, we should take a closer look. Perhaps there are areas we have overlooked. It's like when your car is not running well, the mechanic puts it on the computer to diagnose all of the systems. He might put it up on the lift to inspect the structure of the vehicle. It might be taken on the road for a test drive. Before it could be repaired, it must be properly diagnosed, and any problems discovered. When we are not feeling well, we go to the doctor's office for an exam. The doctor will check our vital signs, maybe do some blood tests, and if things are really serious, do an EKG, MRI, or CT scan. There needs to be a determination made as to the extent of the damage, illness, or problem before there could be a solution

Nehemiah was tasked with the rebuilding of the wall in Jerusalem. He first needed to survey the damage. For three days he went around the city inspecting the wall and the gates. The walls had been destroyed in various places, and the gates had been burned. This took place when God's people had been taken into captivity. But now it was time to rebuild. He needed to identify the breaches in the wall.

Perhaps we have allowed breaches in the walls of our churches. Perhaps there are some practices we have allowed that have weakened the spiritual condition of our fellowship. Maybe the prayer meeting has gone away due to a lack of attendance. There may be many things that have weakened our position. Perhaps entertainment has taken the place of true worship. Maybe church growth has replaced faithful preaching. We need to take a long hard look at any place we might be letting the enemy take a foothold and be willing to repair the breach. Once Nehemiah found the breaches, he set out to fix them. Once the problems are discovered, there should be no delay in fixing them. He called the people together and explained where they were, and where they needed to be. The people responded, "Let us start rebuilding."

Each person or family took the portion of the wall or gates in the immediate vicinity of their own home. The burden was not to be on any one person, or on a few. If each person or family took care of the portion around them, the entire wall would be repaired. Unfortunately, not everyone got involved. There were certain nobles who didn't see the need. They complained about the entire project and wouldn't lift a finger to help. That will always be the case. There will always be a percentage of people who just don't see the need. In a small church, that number seems greater because there are so few people to begin with. But that must never stop us from going forward. There will always be those who say it can't be done, both from within and from without. In Nehemiah's case, he was also plagued by Sanballat and Tobiah, two Samaritan leaders and enemies of Israel. They threatened to reverse any of the progress Nehemiah and God's people might make. Just as we are plagued with the threats of our adversary, the devil. But we must not listen to his voice just as Nehemiah didn't listen to Sanballat and Tobiah. They forged ahead with the project because the people had a heart to work. You can do amazing things with a small number of people who have put their hearts toward God and His church.

I am often amazed at the commitment some people have for the wrong things. I know some people that are truly fanatics for their favorite sports team. If their team is playing, they will stay home from church so as not to miss the game. I use sports as an example, but there are so many things that get people's attention. If we would apply the same commitment and diligence to God's house as we do to our favorite pastime, we would begin to see things turn around.

Proper foundations are essential to solid walls. This is the part that is often overlooked. We focus much of our attention and effort in building on the part that is visible. The most important part of building anything is that which is not seen. If the foundation is not solid nothing built on it will be.

I lived in Baton Rouge, LA for three years while in college. Much of the city barely makes it over sea level. There are many low-lying areas of swampland. One such area was right on the edge of our college campus. But that didn't stop engineers from building a three-story building right where the swamp was. It was amazing to watch the process. They first pumped the standing water away from the swamp and diverted the water supply. Then they filled the area with rock and soil and compacted it with heavy vehicles. But it wasn't ready to be built upon yet. The foundation would not be solid enough to sustain the weight of the building. The engineers drove piles resembling telephone poles into the ground every couple of feet all around the field. When the pressure from the piles being driven into the ground built up, it would cause any remaining water underground to be pressed upward. This continued for several weeks until the engineers were confident all the water had been removed. Now they were able to lay a foundation that would not move. Once the foundation was made sure and steadfast, they were able to build up the walls of the building. Had the builders only looked at the building plans with no concern for the foundation upon which they were building it, the results would have been catastrophic.

Many of the church growth principles fail to consider the foundation of the ministry. The focus is on the visible, tangible, countable aspects of church ministry. I do not deny that there are many good and worthwhile ideas that could be implemented in an effort to see our churches grow. But again I stress the question, upon what foundation are we building?

Before the walls could be replaced, we must make sure we have a solid foundation. It takes a lot of courage to be willing to take a step back to see if there is anything we need to fix. Once we have done the investigating and have determined the repairs we need to make, we must put a plan in place to get it done. Upon what do we plan on building? Will it be the latest church growth concept, or will it be the solid

Word of God? If the walls are going to stand the attacks of the enemy, they had better be built upon the solid foundation of the Word of God. Biblical teaching and not the philosophies of men is the only foundation upon which we could build or rebuild the walls of the church.

Different Vessels

Paul in his second letter to Timothy makes a point regarding vessels in a great house. We understand the *great house* to be the Christian Church. Paul said, "But in a great house there are not only vessels of gold and of silver, but also of wood and of earth; and some to honour, and some to dishonour. If a man therefore purge himself from these, he shall be a vessel unto honour, sanctified, and meet for the master's use, and prepared unto every good work." (II Timothy 2:20-21). He makes the distinction between vessels of gold and silver and those of wood and earth. He makes another distinction between those vessels used for honorable purposes, and those for dishonorable purposes. I realize most commentators assign the honorable purposes to the gold and silver, and the dishonorable purposes to the wooden and earthen vessels. I offer to you my suggestion that this is not necessarily correct.

He does not say that the wooden and earthen vessels have only dishonorable purposes. He simply states that there are different vessels with different purposes. Some are used for honorable purposes and some for dishonorable purposes. To say that wooden and earthen vessels only have dishonorable purposes creates a problem in light of Paul's other teachings. In II Corinthians 4:7, Paul wrote, "But we have this treasure in earthen vessels, that the excellency of the power may be of God, and not of us." Paul clearly teaches that we are all earthen vessels, or vessels of clay (a reference I believe to the jars of clay Gideon used containing the lamps that shown out of darkness causing the defeat of the Midianites – Judges 7). In the context of II Timothy chapter 2, Paul is encouraging Timothy and his readers that if a person purges themselves from "profane and vain babblings" (V.16) they will be a vessel of honor useable by the Master. I use the simile of the vessels to illustrate another point.

There are many vessels in a large house, each one having its own purpose. My aunt used to collect pitchers of all shapes and sizes from all over the world. She had a display case for this collection. On the top shelf were the most prized pieces of her collection. There on the top shelf under the light in the display case, these vessels were visible to all who might enter the room. They were in the most honorable place in her home to be prized and admired. My aunt also has cabinets in her kitchen, and some in her bathroom. Those cabinets also hold vessels of various shapes and sizes. Those in her kitchen are used for the preparation and serving of food, while those in the bathroom are used for hygiene. I'm sure there are additional vessels in her basement and garage with their own intended purposes. Each vessel has its own purpose. I can't imagine she would take a jar, perhaps holding screws, from her garage and place it in her display case. Nor do I think she would take a hand-painted porcelain pitcher from the display case and place it in her basement. Yet each vessel has a place and a purpose. Mealtimes would be nigh impossible were it not for the vessels in her kitchen cabinets. They are not equal in value to her pitchers, but certainly equal in usefulness and I would argue much more so. The pitchers might be prized but serve no useful purpose. The other vessels around her house may not be as valuable in a monetary sense, but they most definitely are valuable in their uses. They are all different vessels with very different uses.

Not all churches are the same. One size most certainly does not fit all. The idea that all churches are supposed to be large churches is a fallacy. Large churches serve a purpose. There may be many purposes, in fact. There are obviously numerous people who find a large church more appealing, and for reasons unique to themselves, more fulfilling. Many people attending large churches would be uncomfortable in a smaller church setting. In the same manner, many people attending small churches would feel lost in a larger church. They are quite content to attend a small church where they enjoy a more intimate fellowship.

Of course, we want to see our ministries grow, as long as that growth is coming from conversions and not migration. But the size of our ministry is determined by the Master and not our strategy. Just as there are different vessels in a house each having its own purpose, so there are different churches each having their own purpose. Instead of trying to be a big church, I believe we should be asking the Lord to show each of us what our purpose is.

Dare to Dream Again

My friend, let me encourage you to dare to dream again. Dreams are an interesting phenomenon. I'm told that everyone dreams every night but not everyone remembers their dreams. Have you ever woken up in the middle of a dream and it was so good you tried to go back to sleep so you could pick up where you left off? Unfortunately, it doesn't seem to work that way.

I thank God He gave us dreams. Scientists haven't been able to explain the purpose of dreams. I believe they are in part given for our entertainment. We all love a good dream. Even the occasional nightmare – some people love horror flicks. I also believe dreams stimulate the nervous system and our emotions which prepare us subconsciously to deal with life's real issues. My beliefs on dreams aside, I want to talk about a different kind of dream - dreams for the future.

One dictionary defines the word *dream* as, "a visionary creation of the imagination… a state of mind marked by abstraction or release from reality." Also, "A strongly desired goal or purpose." The definition of the word *dreamer* is, "One that dreams… one who lives in a world of fancy and imagination… one who has ideas or conceives projects regarded as impractical."[3] Society is cruel and harsh to those who dare to dream; usually, because they have forgotten how to dream themselves. Or they are too afraid to take the risk of following their own dreams. Those people will rob you of your dreams if you aren't careful.

I find three basic ways our dreams are destroyed. First, we blew it. We acted in disobedience to what we knew we should do. We did our own thing rather than obeying God. When we toy with God's plan we wind up in trouble. Samson is a prime example. God called Samson to be a Judge over Israel. He had been separated from his birth to be a Nazarite. But he played fast and loose with the calling of God. He allowed his own lust to dictate his decisions and wound up blind (he lost his *vision*), tied to a millstone doing the work of a mule. Samson's dreams were destroyed by his own doing. (Judges 13-16). Sometimes we let our own desires direct our actions rather than following God's plan. And the dream is gone.

Second, our circumstances change. Through no apparent fault of our own, things change. Perhaps there are those on the Church Board who feel the church should move in a different direction and you're faced with a conflict. Or folks in your church feel things aren't going the way they want them to go, and they leave the fellowship. The church is shrinking, and it seems your dreams have been evaporated. The Apostle Paul knew what it was to be left in the lurch. "At my first answer no man stood with me, but all men forsook me." (II Timothy 4:16). Like Paul, our circumstances changed, and we see our dream slipping away.

Third, someone stole our dream from us. We dared to share our dream with someone else and they robbed us of it. Joseph was a dreamer. He shared his dreams with his brothers regarding what God was going to do. In jealousy, they sold him into slavery, and he wound up in prison on a false accusation (Genesis 37-41). I imagine what must have gone through his mind. "I knew I never should have believed those dreams... I never should have shared them with anyone... I never should have stepped out as I did." It is safer to keep your dreams under lock and key. No one could crush them there. But you will never know what you could have accomplished if you don't dare to dream. Maybe you have dreamed of a strong church where God is moving, and people are coming to faith. But from where you sit it now seems impossible, or at least improbable. Can I dare you to dream again?

I taught my children to never accept a dare. Never allow yourself to be trapped giving someone else control of you. That is in essence what a dare does.

Once a dare is accepted there is seemingly no way out. But there are no dead ends with God.

The Israelites were led to what seemed to be a dead end; Phihahiroth, Migdol, Baalzephon, the Red Sea, Pharaoh's armies (Exodus 14). Moses said, "Fear ye not, stand still, and see the salvation of the Lord, which He will shew to you today: for ye shall see them again no more forever" (V.13).

Samson dared to dream again, and God wrought a great victory through him (Judges 16:30). Paul dared to dream again knowing the Lord stood with him and he was "delivered out of the mouth of the lion." (II Timothy 4:17). Joseph dared to dream again, and he became second in power in all the land of Egypt (Genesis 41:40).

We get so concerned with the passing of time. We see other churches growing, other ministries flourishing, and time keeps passing by. "You don't understand. A lot of time has gone by since I first believed something could happen in my ministry. It's too late." My friend, would you please dare to dream again?

There is one thing we need to understand when we read of great victories in the Bible. From destitution to victory may take us only five minutes to read, but it often represents a lifetime. Noah is undoubtedly one of the greatest characters in the Bible. He was responsible for building the ark which saved mankind from destruction. His entire story is told in four chapters of the Bible, but those chapters represent 950 years, 100 of which were spent building the ark. Jacob dreamed a dream, but it was twenty-two years later that it came to pass. If you had a dream, don't let it go. David was anointed to be king as a young man. Saul tried desperately to kill him to end any chance of David taking the throne. But David knew the will of God for him. He never gave up, and he later became king of Israel establishing his throne in Jerusalem.

If you once had a dream for your church you believed came from God, don't you dare give up! "Now unto Him that is able to do exceeding abundantly above all that we ask or think, according to the power that worketh in us. Unto Him be glory in the church by Christ Jesus throughout all ages, world without end. Amen." (Ephesians 3:20-21)

I hope this writing has been an encouragement to you. If nothing else, perhaps it has just let you know that you are not alone. We have been duped into thinking that we have failed if our churches are not experiencing numerical growth. Writing this has been an encouragement to me because it allowed me to vent many of the frustrations that I have been feeling. The bottom line is that God is the only One who can determine if we are successful.

We could do all the things that the proponents of the Church Growth Movement say we should do and still not see the numbers go up. The Apostle Paul said, "Let a man so account of us, as of the ministers of Christ, and stewards of the mysteries of God. Moreover it is required in stewards, that a man be found faithful." (I Corinthians 4:1-2). Faithfulness is our only responsibility before God. He measures the sincerity of our hearts, and He knows our hearts better than we do (Romans 8:27; I John 3:20).

My final thought. "And again he entered into

Capernaum after some days; and it was noised that he was in the house. And straightway many were gathered together, insomuch that there was no room to receive them, no, not so much as about the door: and he preached the word unto them." (Mark 2:1-2). When Jesus is in the house, the word will get out, and people will come to find Him. We don't need another church growth conference. All we need is Jesus. Just make sure He is in the house.

May God richly bless you and your work for Him.

End Notes

---

[1] Bounds, E.M. Power Through Prayer. Springdale, PA, Whitaker House, 1982

[2] https://WWW.barna.com/research/millennials-oppose-evangelism

[3] Webster's New Collegiate Dictionary. Springfield, MA, G&C Merriam Co., 1979

Made in the USA
Monee, IL
07 July 2026